PlayTime® Piano

Disney

LEVEL 1

Arranged by Nancy and Randall Faber

This to: _____

Production Coordinator: Jon Ophoff
Editor: Isabel Otero Bowen
Design and Illustration: Terpstra Design, San Francisco
Engraving: Dovetree Productions, Inc.

Disney Characters and Artwork © Disney
Disney/Pixar elements © Disney/Pixar

FABER
PIANO ADVENTURES®
HAL•LEONARD®

A NOTE TO TEACHERS

PlayTime® Piano Disney brings together contemporary and classic Disney hits arranged for the Level 1 pianist. In the words of Walt Disney, "There is more treasure in books than in all the pirates' loot on Treasure Island." This book offers musical treasure for piano students with blockbusters from *Coco, The Lion King, Frozen, Mary Poppins, Beauty and the Beast,* and more.

Students develop confidence at the piano through reading notes, intervals, and basic rhythms. *PlayTime® Piano* books explore these music concepts with inspiring songs.

PlayTime® Piano designates Level 1 of the PreTime to BigTime Piano Supplementary Library arranged by Faber and Faber. The series allows students to enjoy a favorite style at their current level of study. PlayTime books are available in these styles: *Popular, Classics, Jazz & Blues, Rock 'n Roll, Ragtime & Marches, Hymns, Kids' Songs, Christmas,* and the *Faber Studio Collection*.

Visit us at **PianoAdventures.com**.

Teacher Duets

Optional teacher duets are a valuable feature of the *PlayTime Piano* series. Although the arrangements stand complete on their own, the duets provide a fullness of harmony and rhythmic vitality. And not incidentally, they offer the opportunity for parent and student to play together.

Helpful Hints:

1. The student should know his or her part thoroughly before the teacher duet is used. Accurate rhythm is especially important.
2. Rehearsal numbers are provided to give the student and teacher starting places.
3. The teacher may wish to count softly a measure aloud before beginning, as this will help the ensemble.

THE PRETIME TO BIGTIME PIANO LIBRARY

PreTime® Piano	=	Primer Level
PlayTime® Piano	=	Level 1
ShowTime® Piano	=	Level 2A
ChordTime® Piano	=	Level 2B
FunTime® Piano	=	Level 3A–3B
BigTime® Piano	=	Level 4 & above

ISBN 978-1-61677-698-5

Printed in U.S.A.

WARNING: The music, text, design, and graphics in this publication are protected by copyright law.
Any duplication is an infringement of U.S. copyright law.

FF3040

TABLE OF CONTENTS

Part of Your World (from *The Little Mermaid*) 4

A Spoonful of Sugar (from *Mary Poppins*) 6

Let's Go Fly a Kite (from *Mary Poppins*) 8

Beauty and the Beast (from *Beauty and the Beast*) 10

Gaston (from *Beauty and the Beast*) 12

Remember Me (Ernesto de la Cruz) (from *Coco*) 16

I Just Can't Wait to Be King (from *The Lion King*) 18

Gummi Bears Theme (from *Adventures of the Gummi Bears*) ... 20

Let It Go (from *Frozen*) 22

Music Dictionary 25

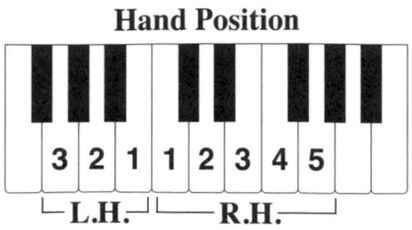

Part of Your World

from *The Little Mermaid*

Music by ALAN MENKEN
Lyrics by HOWARD ASHMAN

WHO SAID THIS?
Flounder, don't be such a guppy.

Moderately fast

mf I wan - na be where the peo - ple are.

I wan - na see, wan - na see 'em danc - in',

walk - in' a - round on those, what - d' - ya call 'em, oh,

Teacher Duet: (Student plays 1 octave higher)

R.H.

L.H.

mp

© 1988 Wonderland Music Company, Inc. and Walt Disney Music Company
All Rights Reserved. Used by Permission.

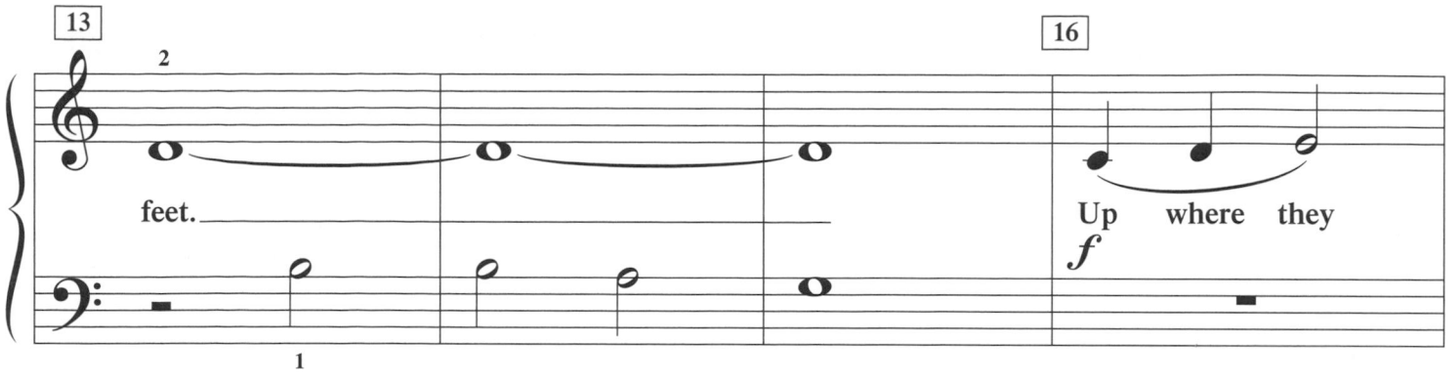

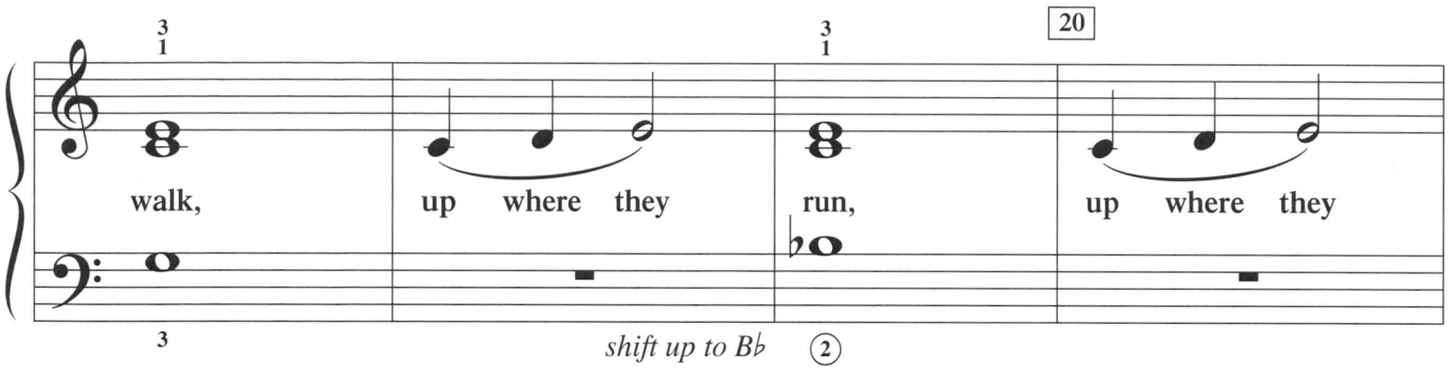

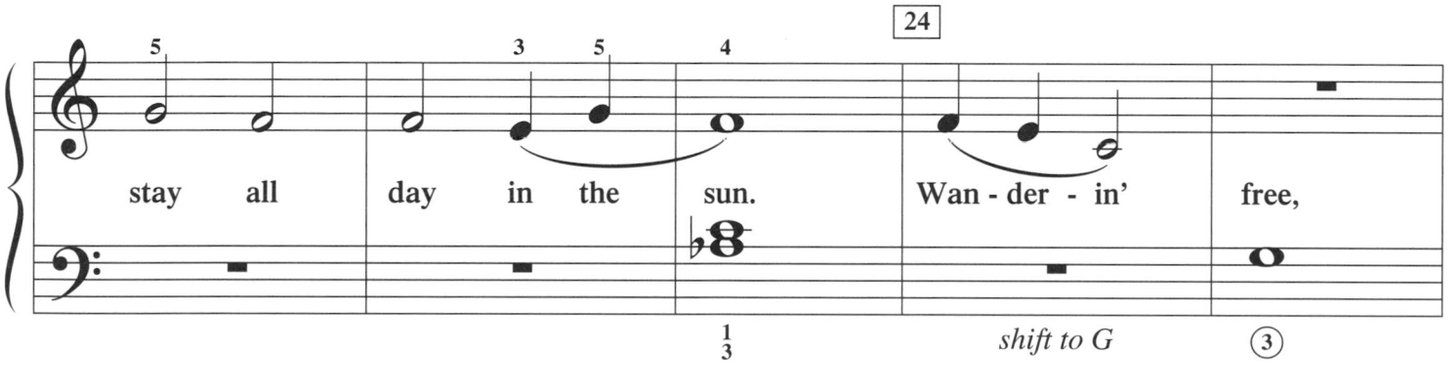

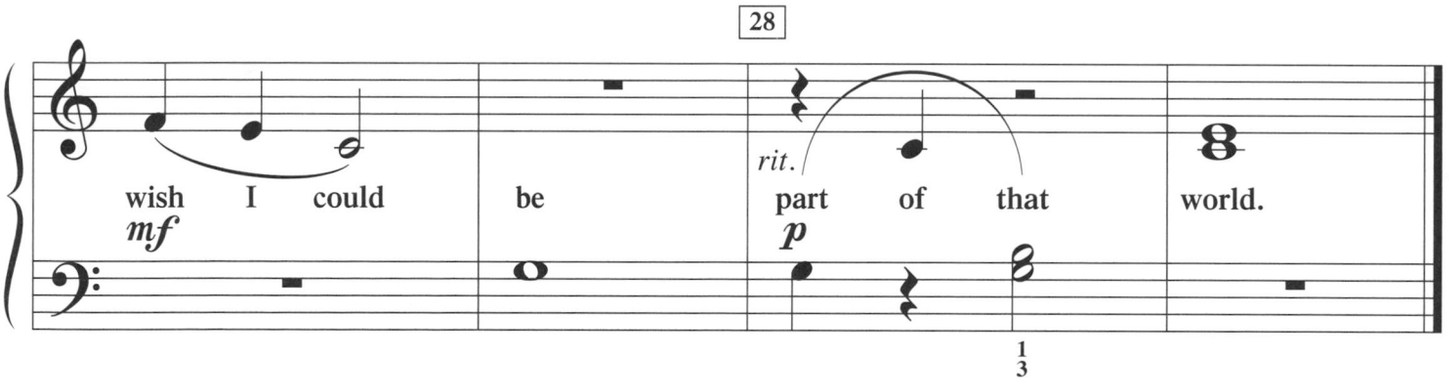

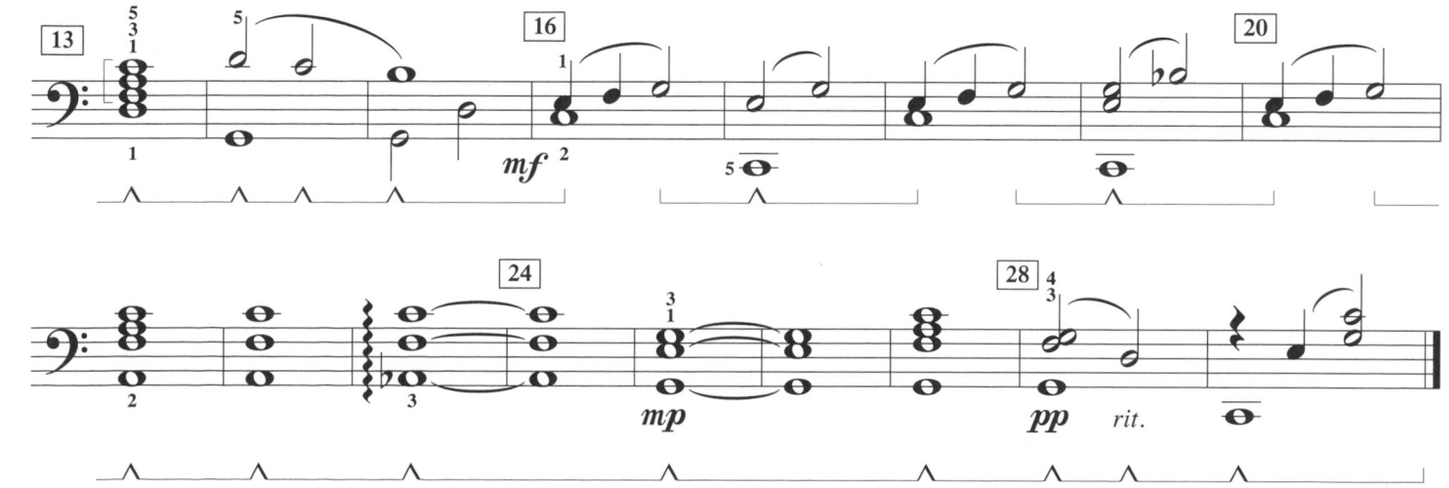

ANSWER: Ariel

© 1963 Wonderland Music Company, Inc.
Copyright Renewed.
All Rights Reserved. Used by Permission.

ANSWER: Michael

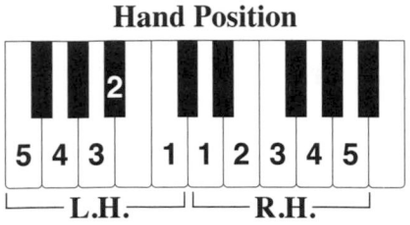

Let's Go Fly a Kite

from *Mary Poppins*

Words and Music by
RICHARD M. SHERMAN
and ROBERT B. SHERMAN

WHO SAID THIS?
Spit-spot!

Moderately fast

mp Let's *(2 - 3)* go *(2 - 3)* fly a kite, *(2 - 3)* up *(2 - 3)*

to the high - est height! *(2 - 3)* Let's *(2 - 3)* go *(2 - 3)*

Teacher Duet: (Student plays 1 octave higher)

R.H.
L.H.
p

cresc.
mf

© 1963 Wonderland Music Company, Inc.
Copyright Renewed.
All Rights Reserved. Used by Permission.

ANSWER: Mary Poppins

© 1991 Wonderland Music Company, Inc. and Walt Disney Music Company
All Rights Reserved. Used by Permission.

ANSWER: Belle

(Contains previously unreleased lyrics from Howard Ashman)

© 1991, 2017 Wonderland Music Company, Inc. and Walt Disney Music Company
All Rights Reserved. Used by Permission.

ANSWER: Gaston

L.H.
34
f slick as Gas - ton, no one's quick as Gas - ton, no one's
38
neck as in - cred - i - bly thick as Gas - ton; for there's
mf
cross 2 over
42
no man in town half as man - ly.
(1 - 2 - 3)
46
(Per - fect, a pure par - a - gon!)
rest
f Who plays
shift LH to A
34 50
mf
38 54
42 58

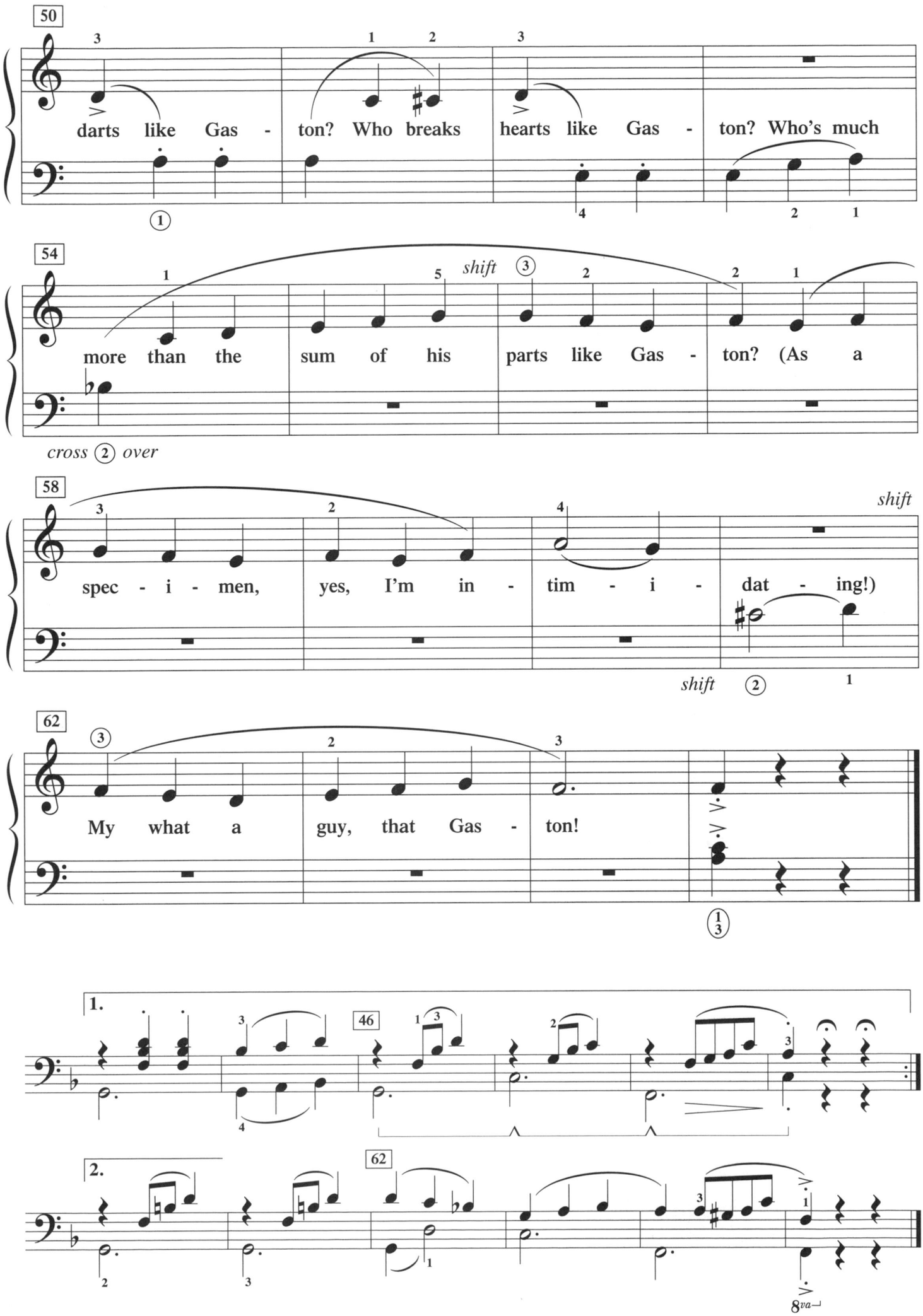
50
darts like Gas - ton? Who breaks hearts like Gas - ton? Who's much
54
more than the sum of his parts like Gas - ton? (As a
shift
cross 2 over
58
spec - i - men, yes, I'm in - tim - i - dat - ing!)
shift
62
My what a guy, that Gas - ton!
1.
46
2.
62
8va

Remember Me
(Ernesto de la Cruz)
from *Coco*

WHO SAID THIS?
I didn't wanna listen, but he was right…nothing is more important than family.

Words and Music by
KRISTEN ANDERSON-LOPEZ
and ROBERT LOPEZ

Moderately

mf Re - mem - ber me, *p* though I have to say good -

bye. Re - mem - ber me, *p* *mf* don't let it make you cry. For

shift e - ven if I'm far a - way I hold you in my heart. I

shift sing a se - cret song to you each night we are a - part. Re - mem - ber

Teacher Duet: (Student plays 1 octave higher)

R.H.

L.H. *mp* *with pedal*

© 2017 Wonderland Music Company, Inc. and Pixar Music
All Rights Reserved. Used by Permission.

ANSWER: Miguel

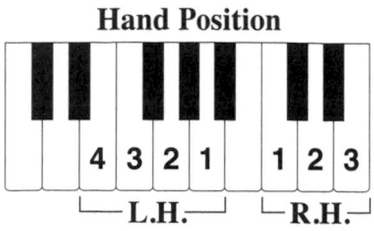

I Just Can't Wait to Be King

from *The Lion King*

Music by ELTON JOHN
Lyrics by TIM RICE

Moderately fast

mf I'm gon - na be a might - y king, so en - e - mies be - ware! "I've nev - er seen a king of beasts with quite so lit - tle hair." I'm work - ing on my roar. "Thus

gon - na be the mane e - vent, like no king was be - fore. I'm brush - ing up on look - ing down. I'm

Teacher Duet: (Student plays 1 octave higher)

R.H.

L.H.

mp

© 1994 Wonderland Music Company, Inc.
All Rights Reserved. Used by Permission.

WHO SAID THIS?
Oh yes, the past can hurt. But the way I see it,
you can either run from it, or learn from it.

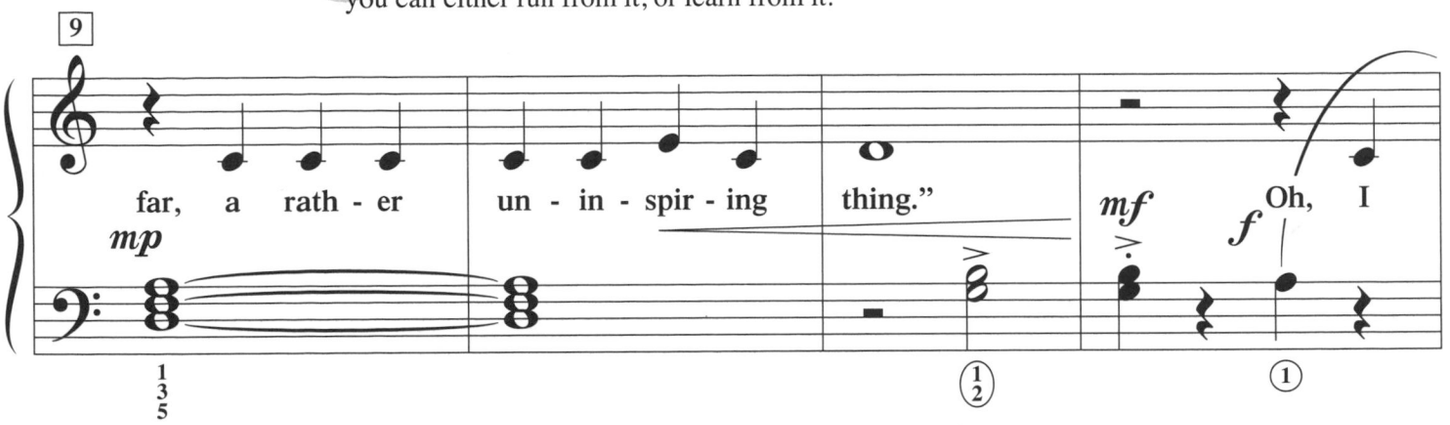

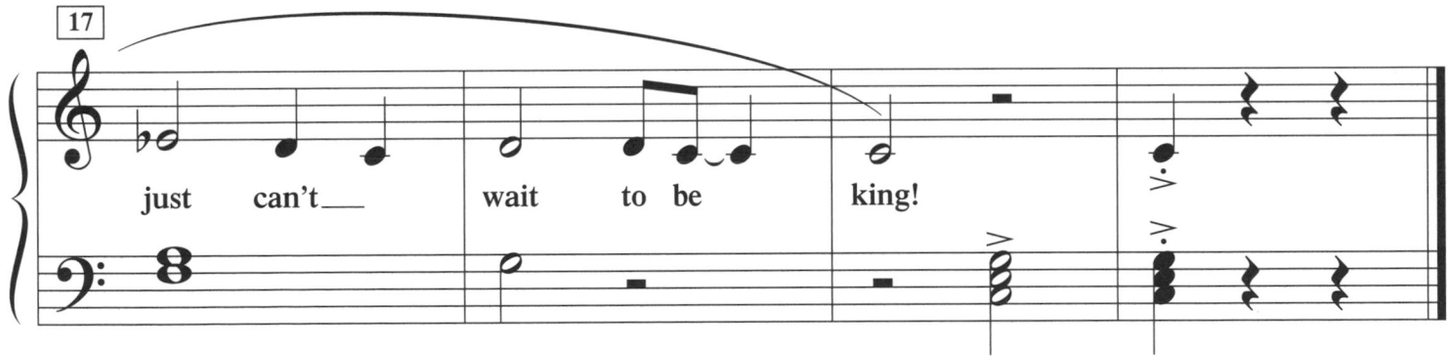

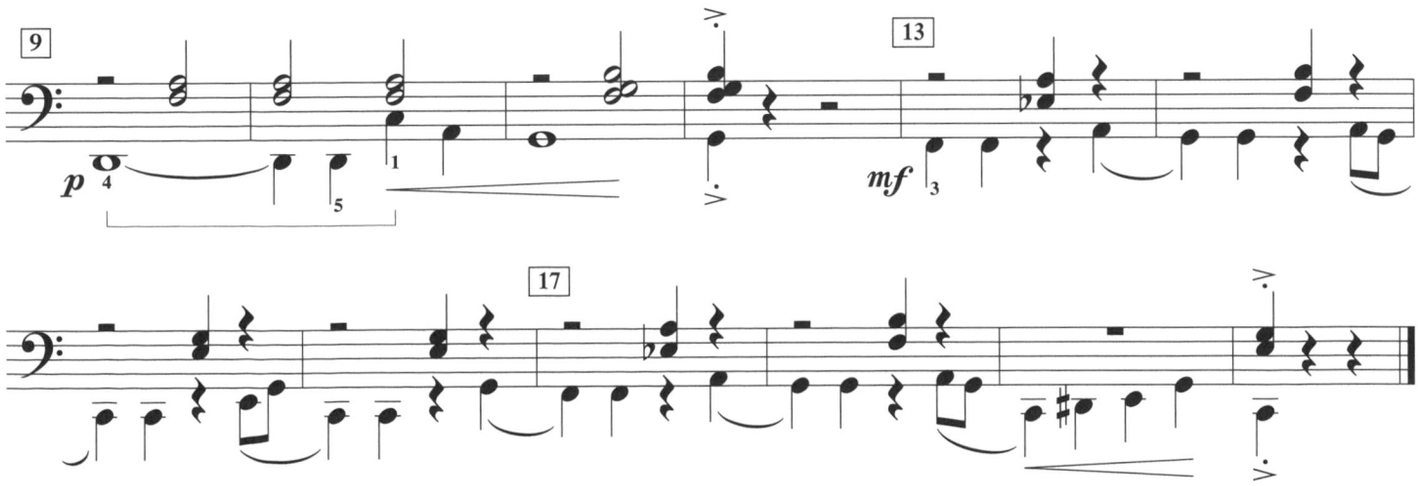

ANSWER: Rafiki

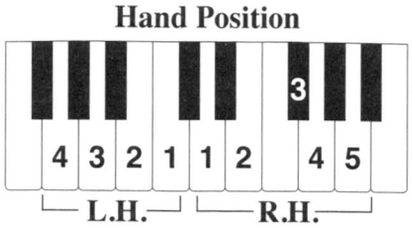

Gummi Bears Theme

from *Adventures of the Gummi Bears*

WHO SAID THIS?
Cubbi, the way to solve problems is to charge right in!

Words and Music by
MICHAEL SILVERSHER
and PATTY SILVERSHER

Happily

mf Dash - ing and dar - ing, cou - ra - geous and car - ing,

5

faith - ful and friend - ly with sto - ries to share.

9

All through the for - est they sing out in cho - rus,

13

march - ing a - long as their song fills the air.

both hands to G Position

Teacher Duet: (Student plays 1 octave higher)

1 9 5 13 1. 2.

R.H.

L.H.

mp

© 1990 Walt Disney Music Company and Wonderland Music Company, Inc.
All Rights Reserved. Used by Permission.

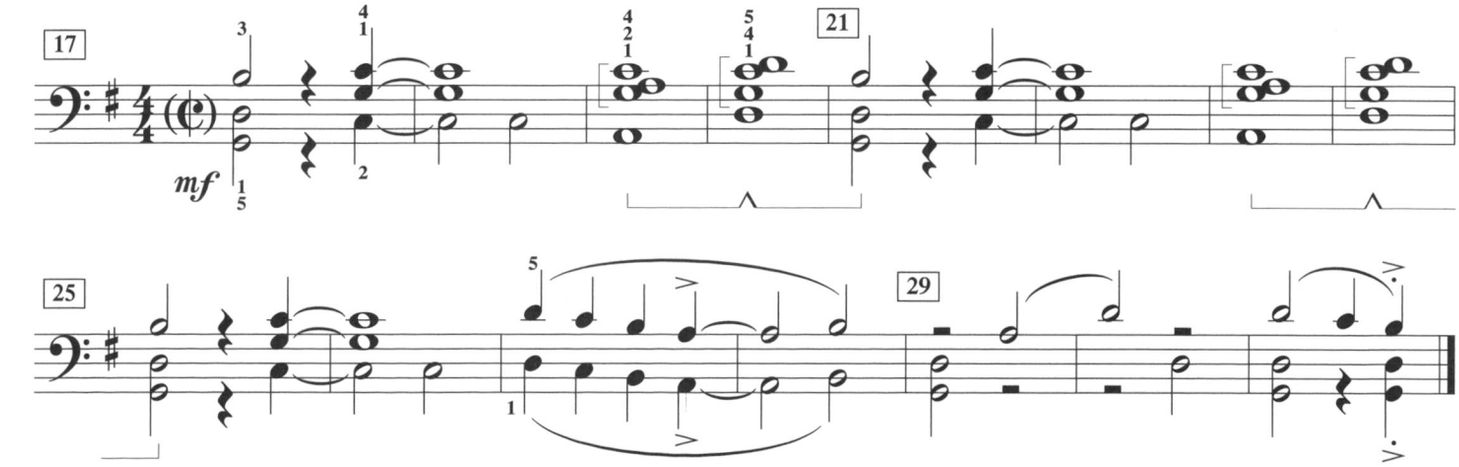

ANSWER: Gruffi

Let It Go

from *Frozen*

Music and Lyrics by
KRISTEN ANDERSON-LOPEZ
and ROBERT LOPEZ

WHO SAID THIS?
You kind of set off an eternal winter…everywhere.

Teacher Duet: (Student plays 1 octave higher)

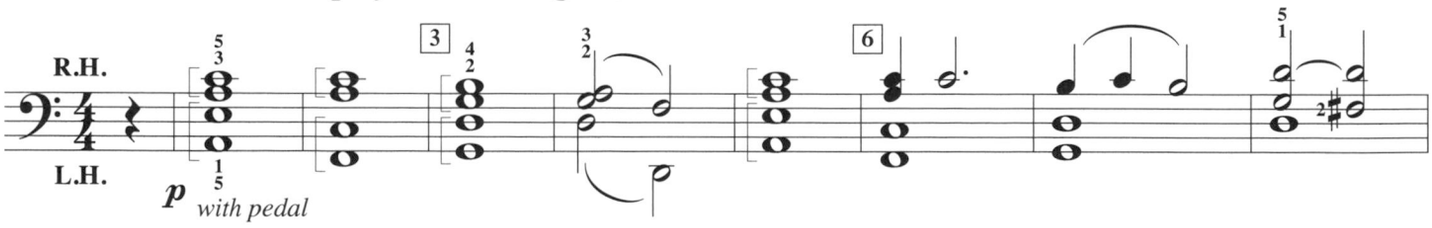

© 2013 Wonderland Music Company, Inc.
All Rights Reserved. Used by Permission.

12
shift to E
side. (2 - 3 - 4 rest) Could-n't keep it in, heav-en knows I've
15
shift to F
tried.
shift both hands to G position!
Let it go,
17
let it go.
(2 - 3)
Can't
19
hold it back an - y - more.
Let it go,
9
12
Let it go,
let it go.
Let it go,
15
19
ANSWER: Anna

21
shift down to E
let it go
Turn a - way and slam the
shift
24
door. (2 - 3 - 4)
I don't care
(1 - 2) what they're
27
going to say.
(1 - 2) Let the
storm rage
on. The
31
cold nev - er both-ered me an - y - way.
rit.
let it go.
21
24
27
31